Cold Stars and Fireflies

Cold Stars and Fireflies

POEMS OF THE FOUR SEASONS

by Barbara Juster Esbensen

Illustrated by Susan Bonners

THOMAS Y. CROWELL   *NEW YORK*

Acknowledgments

"Icicles" appeared in the January 1982
issue of *Cricket* magazine.

"Cardinal," "The Lake," and "December Hills"
appeared in the Winter 1983 issue of *Milkweed
Chronicle: A Journal of Poetry and Graphics.*

Cold Stars and Fireflies: Poems of the Four Seasons
Text copyright © 1984 by Barbara Juster Esbensen
Illustrations copyright © 1984 by Susan Bonners

Designed by Trish Parcell
10 9 8 7 6 5 4 3 2 1

First Edition

Library of Congress Cataloging in Publication Data

Esbensen, Barbara Juster.
  Cold stars and fireflies.

  Summary: A collection of poems about nature and the
changing seasons.
  1. Seasons—Juvenile poetry.   2. Children's poetry,
American. [1. Seasons—Poetry.   2. American poetry]
I. Bonners, Susan, ill.   II. Title.
PS3555.S24C6   1984   811'.54   83-45051
ISBN 0-690-04362-7
ISBN 0-690-04363-5 (lib. bdg.)

This armful of poems is affectionately dedicated to my children—Julie, Peter, Daniel, Jane, George, and Kai

Contents

A Note from the Author

All my life I have been storing up images of weather and the seasons. Years ago I told a friend that I could probably write forever on the theme: "It is snowing." Perhaps this is not quite true, but nevertheless, when I began this book I knew I wanted to write those winter poems first.

No matter that I began to write them during some of the hottest days of a Minnesota summer. No matter that when it came time to begin the poems for the spring and summer sections, snow and frost were thick on the windows of my writing room. I didn't have to be *in* a season to write about it. Time can intensify the way we remember things.

Painters use colors and a brush to put a season on canvas. When I sit down with a clean, white sheet of paper I paint with words.

Like all poets I love to gather words and tumble them about in my mind. I like to watch ordinary words come together in combinations I have never seen before—words we use every day, touching and bursting into small fires along the printed line.

B.J.E.

Autumn

First Day of School

No more barefoot
days.
My feet are clean,
my new socks come up
to my knees.
Inside the school-shoes
my toes are stiff
and afraid of the dark.

The sidewalk is bright
with sun
and holds the old heat
of August
in the cracks.
We can't feel its rough
skin
through our soles now
and it really doesn't know us
anymore.

Questions for September

BLUE! The sky!
How bare and blue
can a sky be?
How high can it stretch
above the trees?

GOLD! The leaves! COPPER!
What are they worth now—
changed into coins
shaking down   one
at   a   time?

Put this sky
and these leaves in a box
in your room
and when winter comes
and you need
this gold   this
blue
and all this copper,
reach in!

Indian Summer

Raise the curtain
on days flaring like trumpets,
branding the air with brassy shouts!

We rake up leaves
and tumble into papery piles
that blaze their colors
high
as the house.

Apples hang like rosy lamps
bronze gongs ring
in the tops of maples.

Smoke begins and smoke stays
in the blue towns.
Around the edges
the enameled sky
is blurred.

This is the beginning.
This is Act One
with the curtain going up
and the stage
on fire!

Exchange

Grey clouds jostle the tops
of maples
and birds scatter up
into the rain.

Red leaves settle
on the pavement
fill the air and the street
with their torn color.

Today the leaves fly south
on rainy wind.
On empty branches
loosely fastened—
sparrows.

Looking Down in the Rain

In the big puddle
at the bus stop
I see the city standing
on its head.

Tops of buildings
move under my boots.
A wavery red light
wiggles
to green.

The school bus
orange as a pumpkin
wobbles in on its roof
and stops.
In the puddle
I see small faces
and yellow leaves *swimming*
under water!

Woolly Bear Caterpillar

Darkness comes early.
The cold, tugging wind pulls it
across the sky—
a billowing cape moving
behind buildings and thin
trees.

Caught up
in the whirling hem
of the wind's skirt
dry leaves spin
over the sidewalk   over
my shoes.
Streetlights blink on.

His rust and black stripes forecasting
winter
the woolly bear ripples
his tickling fur
from one cold hand to   the other.

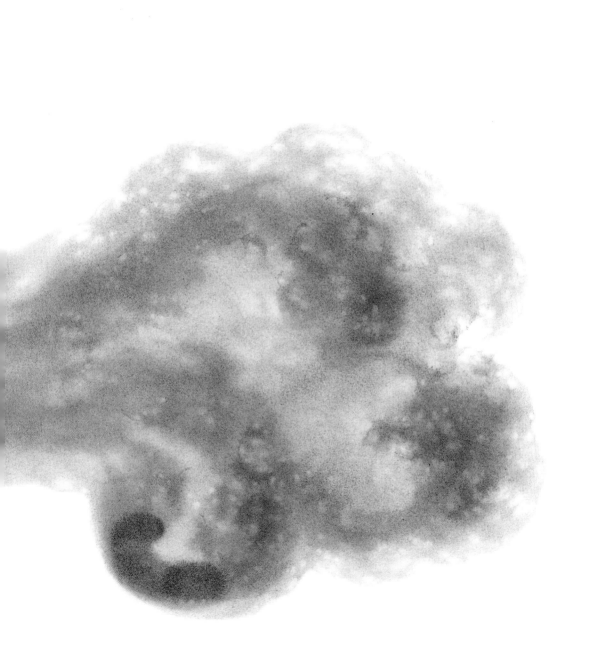

Flyway

FOR ROBERT

A feather lifts
on the wind, and geese
fly in
from silent lakes
to stir the sky
above our field.

The morning air
beats against their thousand
wings.
It fills with their calls.

Now the sky tilts
and the geese pour down—
a heavy ribbon spiraling
into corn rows.

In the evening
under darkening air
the fields will lift up
on the wings of geese
and we will be alone
holding only a feather
against the cold.

Fairy Tale

They don't tell you
it was October when the prince
slammed through the brambles
and pods
over at the castle.
Nobody bothers to mention
the burrs
sticking to the horse's mane
or how the prince's
cat
came out of the hedge-maze
all starred
with milkweed and sticktights.

And it is important
to know
that just before she felt him
kiss her
the princess was dreaming
of hundred-year-old
dandelion-clocks
and that she opened her eyes
to a whirlwind
of white seeds.

A Halloween Ghost Story

Who lurks there
in the dark?
What hollow tribes
shuffle and whisper
from shadow
to shadow   formless
silent
under the ragged moon?

I will not open my door
to them.
No.
They have counterfeited their tongues
to sound like children
crying TRICK OR TREAT!
TRICK OR . . .
NO! I see the pale mask hiding
cold empty eyes.   I see
the wild hair
blowing.   I see the bone
that presses
the bell!

First Snowfall

Out of the grey
pinched air
it falls.

We hear it in the oak trees
hissing
through the brown tongues
of leaves
whispering
and sifting down.

Soon it will erase
the way to school
and our feet will blunder
in blind boots.

Lashes will be fringed
with snowflakes
and our tongues will taste
the cold vanilla
of this early winter day.

Winter

December Hills

White fur
grows thick on the backs
of those green
those brown   those
grassy old animals
the hills.

From their huddled backs
bristle
the spiky hairs
where a few crows roost.

Those old hills
are closing their eyes.
They are putting snowy paws
over their noses.

In white fur coats
they gather themselves together
under the wind
to hurl their stony songs
into the night.

Snow Print One: Mystery

What angel fell here
swinging
his arms into wings
swinging
his big-booted feet
into angel-skirt
frosted with snow?

He's hiding here
somewhere
watching us wonder
which angel fell on his back
in the garden!

Snow Print Two:
Hieroglyphics

In the alley
under the last cold rung
of the fire escape
birds are printing
the new snow
with a narrow alphabet.

Their scribbled secrets
tell of lost songs
and the howling wind
that claws like a cat.

These are messages
from the small dark birds
to me.

Blizzard

On the highway
herded by the wind
cars plow home.

There is no room
for sky or air
the space is filled
with white wings
that beat in thickest
rhythm
soundless and falling.

All night
I will dream of moths
and white birds.

Water runs off those
icicles
barring the tunnel's end,
and in a splash of yellow
the crocus holds her
fingers
to the sun!

Spring

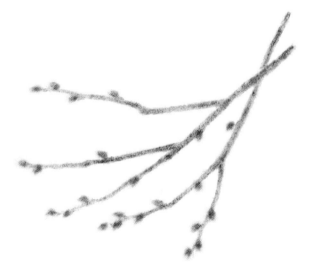

March Twenty-First

Last night
rain filled our dreams,
old snowbanks shrank away
into the ground.

The stiff cold air
softened   spilled thunder
over our roof
rolled thunder
under the house   knocked thunder
against our sleep.

Last night
the soft wet air
opened a river
unlocked a waterfall
splashed our dreams
with rain.

Wake-Up Call

This morning
in all the forests
everywhere
the bears lift their heavy heads
and blink.

They wear hand-me-down
coats
left from some fat, glossy time
they have forgotten—
coats that hang   dusty and loose
the pockets sagging
buttons undone.

On slow legs
still caught in the trap
of winter sleep
the bears shamble
through their open doors.

Wake up, bears!
All the news
is printed on the stones
in green velvet!

Two Ways to Look at Kites

1.
Sky-flowers!
They bloom and toss
on tight stems
invisibly rooted
in our hands.

2.
In the blue air
schools of kites
dive and flash—paper fish!
My kite struggles
to leap free
pulls
my arms out straight
but I reel him in
still fighting   zigzagging
against the currents
of wind.

Wind Stories

Tell me again
about the spring wind   tell me
it is grey
soft at the edges   curling
its tail
around the steeple
purring.

Tell me about the blue gales
that wrestle March
to the ground   the dark
storms shaking rain
out of the night.

I like knowing
the spring wind can pull
rainbows
out of gardens
and fill the windows
of old buildings
with clouds.

Morning

The April day
breaks
into bird-shapes.
Light
flickers along the wings
of sparrows   pours
red and purple
into the fluted bowls
of tulips.

The day
poised on the bluejay's sharp
call
somersaults
all the way to noon
under the songs
of robins!

Now that Spring Is Here . . .

Lift your winter face
your bare arms
up
to the sun.

Tune your ears
to the sound of branches
exploding
their green fire.

Rollerskates chatter
from block to block
in the warm wind   the streets
are noisy and wide again.
Dark tar whispers
under the wheels.

After supper
the sky
will be light.   In the morning
every tree will be tied
with ribbons of melody—
a bright embroidery
of birdsong
to hang from our windows.

May First: Two Inches of Snow

(A Headline)

Yesterday
on the late news
the meteorologist
laughed
drawing those isobars
on the map that makes the weather
happen.

On the map that makes the weather
happen
he put his isobars
right over this town   they weren't
here before.

This laughing meteorologist
just out for a good time
pulled the plug
on the North Pole
and smacked every tulip
and jonquil and lilac
blossom   and windshield
and my face
with snow. Now, REALLY!

Saturday in the Park

Keep this picture—the one
with me stretched out
in the honeyed sun
you holding the balloon,
the sky fragile as violets.
Warm air pours over us,
washes us with the scent
of white bells and fresh loam.

In this picture
I am looking at you
through heavy lashes.
The wind lifts your hair,
the pink balloon bobs above your head.

Just out of sight
the balloon-man
has left the ground,
sways gently
upward.

Light spray from the fountain
wets our faces.
I can't recall who took this
picture . . .

Spring Fever

We don't remember   we weren't
paying attention
when the sun's hot
thumbs
first pried us loose
from shoes and socks   when
that first warm breath
pulled off our hats
and sailed them away.

All at once
awnings snapped open their
welcome shade.   Our blood
brightened   beat quick-time
and climbed like sap does
beneath the bark.

Trees edged forward
testing this throbbing pulse
with new fingers.

Wild
we ran   our bare feet
playing the hot cement
like drums   our throats
open
and singing.

Spring Cleaning

Notice how
after this rain   the trees
combed all the tangles
from the sky   and how the sun
with warm rough hands
flipped each cold blue shadow
to its green side
fringed with dandelions.

New leaves press their oval
shadows on my walls   thumbprints
the aproned wind
rubs out.

Last Day of School

Look out!
If you aren't careful
it will happen like this: Someone
will say the word
and that
word
will catapult you   down
the halls   out
the doors   and into
a serious collision
with
SUMMER!

Summer

June

Everything is light
everything poised
a little above
the day.

Beneath our feet
the earth breathes   lazy
weighted
with the heavy freight of roses.

Our hands fill
with blue and gold parcels:
hours that unwrap and ride out
on butterfly wings
or crawl leisurely
bending a single stalk of grass.

We have earned it—this gift
of days torn slowly
from the long calendar.

At the Pool

This summer we dare—we climb   we
dive from the highest
place   shatter the emerald
water   the sun's net
flickers on our bodies
catches our shouts.

We are seals! Porpoises!
Silver bubbles form
in our tumbling wake
cling
to our seal-whiskers   our
porpoise-tails.

The clear green water
is our world
until lungs explode us
into air.

Fourth of July

Tonight the air explodes!
Sparkling fragments burn
and scatter.   Fire cascades
falls   pours into the dark
like water.

Dazzled by bomb-burst
we lift our faces
to the spangled sky.   We are
fire-worshippers. Our one long breath
is AHHHHHHH
and OHHHHHHHHH.   Our eyes reflect
the blazing seeds
that drift on the wind
and sputter out.

Walking home
we have the cold stars
and fireflies
tangled in the grass.

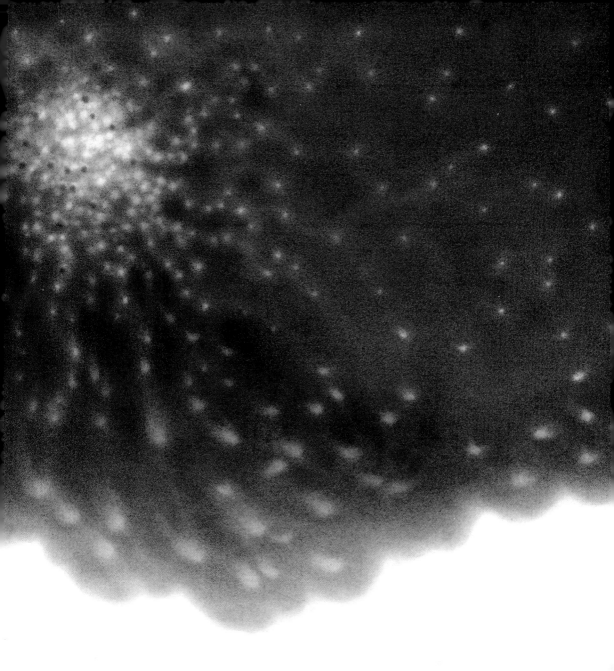

Drought

Our blue planet
tipped at a crazy angle
toward the sun
lit
this invisible fire.

Clear flames waver
over the city   buildings
bend in the heat   trees
wilt
their skin hot   feverish.

In alleys the birds
wash in sunblaze
and dust.

The sky is empty of everything
we yearn for:

        cloud

        mist

        the rain's perfection.

Out beyond the edge of town
hot   dry
the dying corn prays
in the fields.

Storm

There has never been a wind
like this   seething
through trees   twisting
the thin neck
of every leaf   a force
from nowhere
let loose over our heads.

There's been a mistake   these
aren't clouds   these purpling mounds
bulging up
into thick afternoon air   these
are monstrous heads that grow
and change   advance
on misshapen bodies
climbing over the horizon.

The rain comes—a fist in the mouth!
Dust jumps under the beating   turns
into mud and races downhill.

This is an attack   a battering
Take off your shoes!   Hang on to my
hand!   Like Noah's children
we wait
for a dove
and a rainbow.

Mud

Your fingers can take
mud
or leave it   your hands
can roll mud
into a ball   shape it
punch it   slap
it down on a hot sidewalk
bake it

Your toes know
mud
when they see it   they
want to step into it   wet and cool
and smile
ten
    wiggling
       muddy
         smiles!

Walking Past the School
at Night

It lies
solid   stretched out
eyes blank   a blind
beast
dozing in the glare
of moonlight.

Under the dusty hide
heartbeats echo
in the hollow chest   pulse
has slowed to
nothing   the clanging bell
around its neck
is still.

We hurry past   staring at
each other   something
is moving!   A shadow?
Did you see an eye
blink?
A hot wind blows—breath of
the mammoth!
Run!

Campsite

Something points us
here   a little
rise of ground   sentinel
hill
between the forest and the shore

Loons call out   flint chips
catch the sky's last
light   someone finds
an arrowhead   a broken clay
pipe

The earth
scorched by ancient fires
waits for our ring
of stones   our smoke and blaze
Something brought us here

We move into firelight
and out   faces lit and
shadowed   lit
and shadowed   the stones glow
the flames die   we stir wild sparks
into the night

Into the firelight and out
they move
we almost see them
bent in soundless dance   lit
and shadowed   their eyes see
us   the arrowhead   our
wild sparks   Something
wants us here . . .

Perseid Meteor Shower

Every summer, around August 12, you
can expect to see more than 65 meteors in
an hour of watching the late night sky.
They stream toward us from the
constellation PERSEUS.

Unfastened
whizzing between the steady stars
and the lake
meteors streak the night
skid   silver on the sky

Obsidian mirror   the lake
holds us   keel-to-keel—
paper cut-outs scissored against
starshine

Stirred by my paddle
the stiff geometry
of constellations
trembles
on black water

In the story   Perseus
saw Medusa's face   her snake-hair
in his polished shield
He did not turn to stone   He
cut off her head   its writhing curls
still hissing

We will not turn
to stone   watching
in our lake-mirror   how
the ancient snakes break loose and fall
still hissing . . .

Nocturne for Late Summer

*A rather accurate measure of Fahrenheit
temperature can be made by adding 37 to
the number of chirps a cricket makes in
15 seconds.*

Hot   languid
the still days roll over us
but the dark comes earlier
now.

In the rubble near the playground
fence
one cricket tunes
his fiddle.   Begins

Under a sky the color of opals
he is playing *allegro*.
Adding thirty-seven
he heats up the night to ninety
degrees.

Soon the winds will swing
north. Somewhere a yellow leaf
edged with red
already hides in green branches.

Crickets will play
their *andante* cadenza
for fifteen bars   add thirty-seven

The leaf
      will
            fall . . .

Index of First Lines